SMEP

SOMERSET MUSIC
EDUCATION PROGRAMME

GROWING WITH MUSIC

2

Michael Stocks
Andrew Maddocks

LONGMAN

Choppety Chop

Do you know 'Chop, chop, choppety chop'?

Tap these heartbeats, and feel the pulse as you sing:

1	2	3	4
♩.	♩.	♪ ♪ ♪	♩.
Chop,	chop,	chop -pe - ty	chop
tai	tai	ti - ti - ti	tai

1 Ask a partner to tap the pulse while you sing the whole song.

2 Tap the heartbeats (the pulse) and sing the song with your 'thinking' voice.

chop, chop...

3 Ask a partner to tap the pulse while you speak the rhythm of the song, using rhythm names.

tai, tai, ti-ti-ti tai.

The axe falls and rises in time with the pulse.

$\begin{array}{c} 6 \\ 8 \end{array}$

| Chop, | chop, | chop-pe - ty chop, | Chop off the bot-tom and | chop off the top. |

On 'choppety', see how the beat divides into three.

In the third bar, both beats divide, so that
there are six notes in the bar.

Sing, or say, the poem.
Chop the beats with your hand as you sing.

Speak the rhythm names, and chop the strong beat
in each bar.

p.66 **3**

Skippety Skip

In this poem there are two beats to each bar:

Skip - pe - ty skip,
Pep - per and salt,

skip - pe - ty skip,
pep - per and salt,

Un - der and o - ver with ne - ver a slip,
O - ver and un - der with ne - ver a halt.

Some beats are divided into three notes.
Some beats have just one note.
Tap the rhythm of the poem.

With a partner, choose different percussion instruments.
One of you play the pulse, the other play the rhythm.
Then change round.

p.67

Here are three more rhythms to perform.

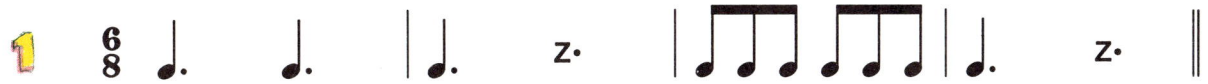

Choose a steady tempo.

First **speak**, then **tap**, each rhythm.

1   $\frac{6}{8}$ 𝅗𝅥. 𝅗𝅥. | 𝅗𝅥. z. | ♫♫♫ ♫♫♫ | 𝅗𝅥. z. ‖

2   $\frac{6}{8}$ 𝅗𝅥. z. | 𝅗𝅥. z. | 𝅗𝅥. ♫♫♫ | ♫♫♫ 𝅗𝅥. ‖

The second player starts when the first player reaches here.

Rhythm 3 can be performed as a canon. You will need a partner to do this.

Use two different percussion instruments.

3   $\frac{6}{8}$ 𝅗𝅥. 𝅗𝅥. | *♫♫♫ 𝅗𝅥. | ♫♫♫ ♫♫♫ | 𝅗𝅥. z. ‖

Six-eight challenge

Now make up a 4-bar rhythm piece in $\frac{6}{8}$ using ♩. and ♪♪♪ and 𝄾.

Speak it,  tap it,  and play it on an instrument.  Then write it down.

ti-ti-ti tai

Ask a partner to speak, tap and play your new rhythm.

Here is a two-part rhythm in $\frac{6}{8}$:

Work with a partner.
Speak, then tap, the upper part.
Speak, then tap, the lower part.
Then perform the piece together,
in two parts.

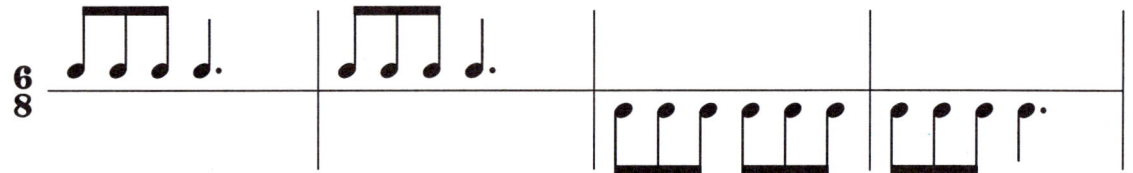

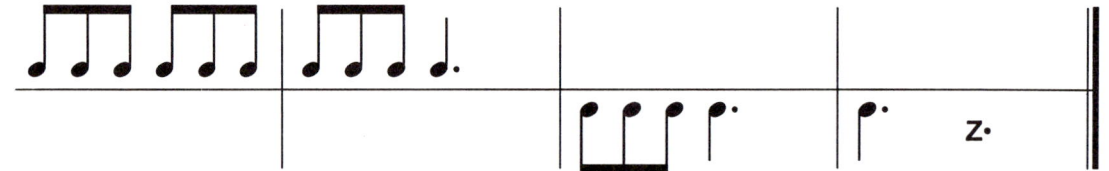

Try performing it with two different percussion instruments.

6 p.67 ✏ 6

Here are two songs you know.
Sing the melodies.

Song 1 (6/8):
r | d | r m r d | r r s m r d | r r s m |
r r s m r d | r r s m | r | d | r m r d ||

Song 2 (6/8):
m r d r | m r d r | m r d r | m r m s |
m r d r | m r d r | s s s s s | s s s s ||

Only two of the pictures match the songs. Which two?

Play these melodies **from memory** on a keyboard
or other instrument, with doh = G.

Which notes do you use?

A new rhythm

♥　　♥　　♥　　♥

Hi - cko - ry,　di - cko - ry,　| dock,　　　z　　♪
The

mouse　ran　up　the | clock.　　　z　　(♪)

This is a very 'bouncy' rhythm.

ta　ti　ta　ti

1 Say the whole poem to your partner.

...... mouse ran up the clock.

2 Ask your partner to speak back the rhythm in rhythm names.

.....ta ti ta ti tai

3 Using a writing sheet, write the rhythm of all the poem.

1 Tap a pulse and speak the rhythm names.

ti-ti-ti ti-ti-ti

2 Choose a percussion instrument and play each rhythm piece twice – first slowly, and then in a faster tempo.

Now make your own rhythm, including ♩♪.

Speak it, tap it and play it on an instrument.

Write down your new rhythm.

Ask a partner to speak, tap and play your new rhythm.

Tap the rhythm before singing:

Notice the phrase marks. There are two phrases.

Now look at this new rhythm.

Speak it and tap it.

Choose singing names (l–s–m–r–d) for each phrase.

Write your melody down in rhythm-solfa.

Play your melody, from memory, on a keyboard or other instrument (doh = C).

Here is the double-decker Song Bus again.

The passengers always sing in two parts.

Sing this two-part piece with a partner.

Then change parts and sing it again.

When you know it well, make small changes to the melody as you sing;
perhaps change the rhythm a little, or the singing names.

Can you improve the piece this way?

p.70

Melody detective

This melody has two phrases:

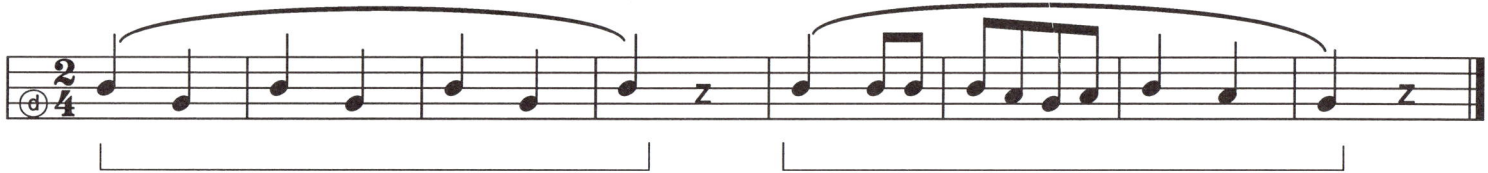

This is phrase A.

This is called phrase B
because it is different.

This melody has four phrases:

A	A	B	C
s m d m s s s s	s m d m s s s s	r d r m	d d d d

Phrase 2 is the same as phrase 1, but phrases 3 and 4 are different.

Therefore the phrase pattern is A A B C.

What is the phrase pattern for
this melody?

r d r m r d · r r s m r d r r s m · r r s m r d r r s m · r d r m r d

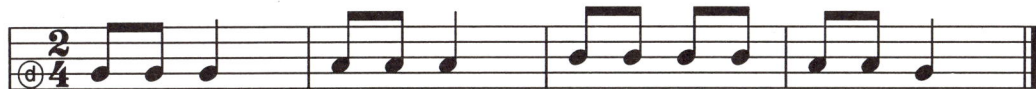

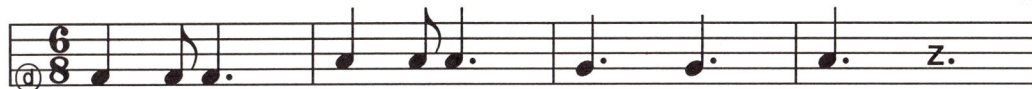

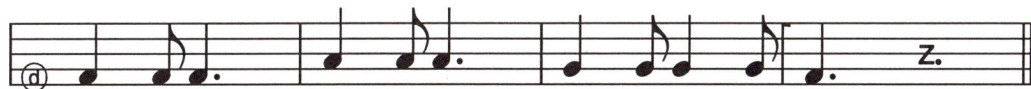

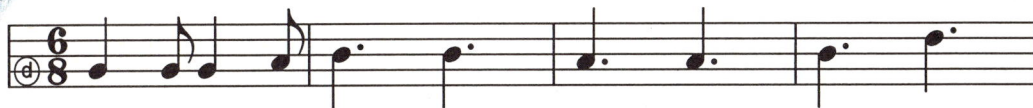

Can you sing
these melodies?

Do you know the words
to any of them?

p.72 13

Sing this melody:

Look at it closely.
It is almost a *me–ray–doh* melody, but it has one *soh*.

Can you point to the *soh*?

Can you find a melody with *soh* on page 13?

You have learned five notes so far
(*lah, soh, me, ray, doh*).
But some melodies use only three or four of these notes.

Which notes does this melody use?

Compose four-bar melodies in $\frac{2}{4}$ or $\frac{6}{8}$ using these groups of notes and writing in staff notation.
(i) s-m-r (ii) m-r-d (iii) s-m-d

Write each melody with ⓓ in a new position each time.

Out of our five notes
(*lah*, *soh*, *me*, *ray*, *doh*),
this melody uses three.

Which notes does it use?

The next melody uses four
of our five notes.

Which notes does it use?

Compose four-bar melodies in $\frac{2}{4}$ or $\frac{6}{8}$
for each of these note groups:

(i)   l–s–m–d
(ii) l–s–r–d

Write your melodies in staff notation,
with ⓓ in a new position each time.

You will need to space your bar lines
wider apart when writing in $\frac{6}{8}$.

Here are two melodies:

Do they both have ⓓ in the same position?

Which melody has three phrases?
How many phrases does the other melody have?

Do they both begin on *doh*?

Do they both end on *doh*?

Can you compose an eight-bar melody in $\frac{2}{4}$ time, using l-s-m-r-d? Write it in staff notation.

16 p.72 8

These two rhythms look different:

♫ ♪ ♪

But they are only written differently.
They are the same rhythm.
Two **eighth notes** can be joined together or written separately.

Perform this:

Then ask your partner to perform this:

They should sound the same.

In the next example, some of the
separate eighth notes (♪)
have been replaced by an eighth note
rest (ｷ).Now we have a changed rhythm:

While your partner taps a steady pulse,
improvise a short rhythm, trying to
include the eighth note rest (ｷ).

Ask your partner to repeat the
rhythm you made, and
then write it for you to perform.

Musical trains

Two of these InterCity trains waiting at the station are full of melody.

With a tapped pulse, speak the rhythm names of each melody. Then, tap the rhythm with one hand and the pulse with the other.

Read and sing the melodies. Tap a steady pulse.

Make a short 'mm' for each eighth note rest (𝄽).

Draw your own train and then fill it full of rhythm.

Make up a rhythm piece to include ♪ and 𝄽 .

Here is a new rhythm: ♪ ♩ ♪
It uses the separate eighth note.

It is called a 'syncopated' rhythm.

$\frac{2}{4}$ | ♪♪ ♪♪ | ♩ ♩ | ♪♪ ♩ | ♪ ♩ z ‖

s s s l | s m | d d | d d

Hill an' gul - ly ride a, Hill an' gul - ly.

This engine is delivering ♪ ♩ ♪ rhythms to the station.

♪ ♩ ♪

Two more musical trains are waiting to leave.

$\frac{2}{4}$ ♪♪ ♩ | ♪♪ ♩ | ♪ ♪♪ ♩ | ♩ z

$\frac{2}{4}$ ♪♪ ♩ | ♪♪ ♩ z | ♪♪ ♩ | ♪ ♪♪ ♩

Try them out, with a partner tapping a steady pulse.

Melody trials

Sing these two melodies and learn them by heart.

Play them **from memory** on a keyboard
or other instrument, with doh = C.

Choose one of them for a friend's birthday.
Add suitable words to it.

Or perhaps you would rather write your own melody.

Make a l–s–m–r–d melody from the rhythm below.
Write your melody in rhythm-solfa.

p.74 7

This page has three new two-part pieces for you to sing with your partner.

Counting up

This train is called a *mono*rail.
It runs on *one* line.

This melody is on a *mono*tone.
It uses only *one* note.

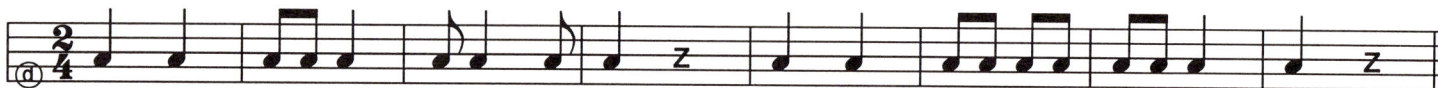

A *bi*cycle has two wheels.

This melody is made from a *bi*chord – it uses only two notes.

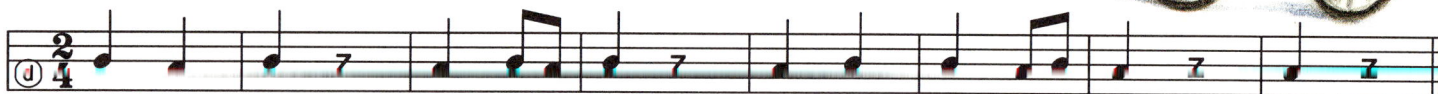

Perhaps you can make an interesting bichordal melody.
A bichord moves by step, so you need notes which
are next to each other, for example *me* and *ray*.

Write your bichordal melody in staff notation.

Ask a partner to sing your melody to you.

A camera is on a tripod. A tripod has <u>three</u> legs.

How many corners does a <u>triangle</u> have?

How many notes does a <u>trichordal melody</u> have?

Here is a trichordal melody; read and sing it with a partner.

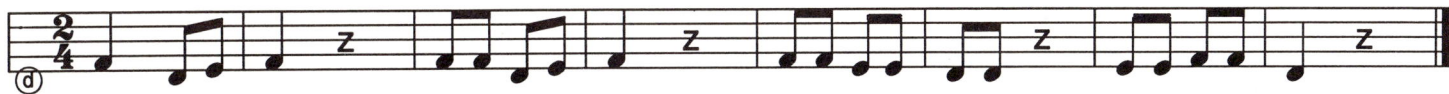

Here is another trichordal melody; read and sing it with a partner.

Compare the two trichordal melodies.

How are they the same?

How are they different?

Perhaps these ideas will help:

time signature!

phrase patterns!

phrase lengths!

rhythm elements!

repetitions!

p.76

Here is a trichordal melody.
Sing it to solfa, as you tap the pulse.

It has the following features: $\frac{6}{8}$ time signature · two phrases · needs a gentle tempo · uses me, ray, doh.

Here is another trichordal melody.

It has the following features: $\frac{2}{4}$ time signature · three phrases · needs a quick tempo · uses me, ray, doh.

Compare the two melodies.

Compare the two melodies.
Which features are the same?
Which are different?

Use the trichord (*me*, *ray*, *doh*) to compose two melodies of different character.

Decide which features will be the same.
Decide which features will be different.

Write your melodies in staff notation.

24 p.76 8

Sing this melody with a partner:

It has a new fourth note, called *fah*.

Melodies with four notes (*fah*, *me*, *ray*, *doh*) are using the *tetra*chord.

('tetra' = 4).

With your partner, practise singing the notes of the tetrachord (f–m–r–d). Use handsigns to help.

Working with a partner, improvise short tetrachordal phrases to each other, and see if the other can recognise *fah*:

– improvise a melody which moves by step;
– improvise a melody which 'jumps'.

Here is a tetrachordal piece in staff notation,
arranged in two parts:

All night long, ev - 'ry hour, chime the bells from yon - der tow'r

a - ring - ing, a - ring - ing.

All night long, ev - 'ry hour, chime the bells from yon - der tow'r, a - ring - ing, a ring - ing.

Sing both parts to solfa with your partner,
looking for the new note *fah*.

Using solfa, now sing it as a duet, one person singing
the upper part, the other singing the lower.

Can you sing it as a duet, using the words?

26 p.77

In a *pent*athlon, athletes take part in *five* events.

A *pent*agram is a *five*-pointed star.

The *pentachord* has *five notes* (*soh*, *fah*, *me*, *ray*, *doh*).

Here is a pentachordal melody:

$\frac{2}{4}$ m m m r | d | d | r r r f | m r d | s s s f | m | m d | r r m r | d | z ‖

Using the white notes only of a keyboard instrument, play the doh pentachord on C.
On which note other than C can you build another doh pentachord using the white notes only?

Sing the above melody to solfa from memory.

Using your memory, play the melody on the keyboard instrument, using the white note pentachords you have found.

p.79

Four beats to a bar

Here is a doh pentachordal melody in staff notation:

Once a man fell in a well,   splish, splash, splosh, he soun-ded.   If he had not fal-len in,   He would not have drown-ded.

Sing it to solfa, then sing it with the words.

This melody has four quarter notes to each bar.

Therefore, its time signature is $\frac{4}{4}$.

Working with a partner, one person sings the melody (solfa or words);

Once a man fell in a well...

one... ....two..

the other taps the pulse, and counts out loud the four beats in each bar.

Compose four bars of rhythm in $\frac{4}{4}$, repeating certain rhythm patterns if you wish.

Write down your rhythm, and ask a partner to perform it on a drum.

p.81   6

A new kind of note:

It is called the half note.

With your partner, sing this two-part piece to discover how the new half notes should be performed:

Sing this melody:

Quickly

The two dots at the end mean *repeat*.

Now compose a melody (using s–f–m–r–d) which repeats, like the one above, and which uses the new half note.
Write it down in staff notation.

Write some words for your melody.

A string of *six notes* is called a *hexachord*
(lah/soh/fah/me/ray/doh).

With a partner, practise the handsigns for these six notes.
Practise large 'jumps', and listen carefully so
that the intervals are accurate and in tune.

This hexachordal melody is in staff notation:

Compose an A B A B melody in 4/4 using the
doh hexachord.

Write the finished melody in staff notation.

Add words, to make a song about school holidays.

Perhaps the rhyming pattern of the words could
also be A B A B

Setting words to music

Here is a poem:

The rhythm is written above the words.

Write down the rhythm (use Writing Sheet 7), and compose a melody for these words.

Use the doh pentachord, and use an A B C A phrase pattern.

Next, write your melody in staff notation (Writing Sheet 8), with *doh* in the bottom space of the staff.

Ask a partner to perform your song.

Have a class concert to perform the songs you have written.

Look at this poem:

Run round the sandhills,
Chase after me.
Run to the water's edge,
And paddle in the sea.

Compose a melody for the poem.

It could be in $\frac{4}{4}$ or in $\frac{6}{8}$.

Write your rhythm above a staff (Writing Sheet 8).

Now think about the structure of your melody; the rhyming pattern might help you decide.

Using the doh hexachord, compose a melody based on your rhythm.

doh
doh, soh
doh?

It is a good idea to use your 'thinking' voice as much as possible when you compose melodies.

Write your melody in staff notation, with *doh* on the second line up.

Perhaps the class could select three versions of the song for performance in school assembly.